From an Armchair in Kent

A poetic commentary

by

Ron Sims

From an Armchair in Kent

Published by Lulu

Year of publication 2007

Foreword by Tim Harris

Cover Illustration by Sally Harris

ISBN 978-1-84799-257-4

www.fromanarmchairinkent.co.uk

www.lulu.com

For June

Contents

Foreword

As a boy my memories of my Grandad fit mainly into two topics; walking long distances while I talked and he listened (I assume); and him sitting in his favourite armchair with paper in hand, whether he was awake or not.

When I wasn't talking he would regale me with stories of when he was younger; dispensing advice for me to be as successful as him, although too modest to admit that he fitted that category.

"It doesn't matter what you know, if you know enough to earn a shilling," he would say. A phrase I didn't really understand until I was older, having been born after decimalisation, but now I've been working for 6 years something I know to be true. If only a shilling was enough to live on these days!

"Communication and people is the key to success." My Grandad got on with everybody and anybody, and never held a grudge. Large numbers of friends and family often came to visit for a cuppa and a chat, and perhaps he never quite realised how popular he was.

It was when we were visiting my grandparents flat as a family that I realised the importance of my Grandad's armchair. I often tried to jump into the prized seat, but was almost always evicted. It was from this chair that he made observations on the world; of anything from our family to the royal family and everything in between.

In his later years he was joined at times in his armchair by the smartest of canine friends; a dog called Buttons who belongs to my Auntie Annabel. He would jump up (or be lifted) into the seat alongside Grandad where they would sit and watch the comings and goings together, knowing they shared the best seat in the house. They say that animals are instinctive; I wonder if Buttons knew the secret to my Grandad's success was his armchair in Kent.

Tim Harris

(Grandson number 3 and Rumm'un)

About the Author

Ronald Malcolm Sims, Ron or Simmo to his family and friends, was born the middle son in a family of 5 brothers in Burham in Kent in 1929. In 1949 he married June and went on to have three children, Julie, Don and Annabel, who in turn all married and produced six grandchildren (and a grand dog).

A carpenter by trade, he worked his way up from apprentice to building site manager over his working life, winning awards for his building work. He also served for a brief time in the RAF.

Towards the end of his life he lived in a garden flat in Royal British Legion Village, and it is here that he wrote most of his poems.

This book was published after his death in 2007 but is in keeping with what he would have done had he published it himself.

Introduction

A Secret Ambition

Since a very early age I have always had a hankering to write, indeed it was even forecast by my elementary schoolmaster that I would be a writer of renown one day. This ambition or this need even, I have carried with me for the greater part of my life.

Instead of going on to further education at a grammar or mathematical school it was deemed that I should leave school at fourteen and become apprenticed to a trade.

Apart from writing compositions and playing football and cricket, my only other worthwhile attribute was at woodwork. So my father in his wisdom, said I ought to become a carpenter and joiner in the building trade.

One has to bear in mind that the period of time I am talking about is nineteen forty three, there was a war on and most children of working class parents left school at fourteen. One must also remember that there was no such person as a careers officer or teacher, so right from the word go we had to rely on our own initiative and determination to find employment of any kind.

Looking back over the years to my school days at a little village elementary school, I can't help but think that it may have been planned that the majority of us children should only be educated to a level sufficient to either work in a local paper mill, which by the way was a very flourishing local industry then, a labourer on one of the many farms in the area or if you were lucky, like I was, become apprenticed to a trade.

I eventually finished my apprenticeship and duly became a carpenter, although in the early days the work consisted mainly of repairing bomb damage to all kinds of buildings from churches and shops to the smallest of cottages, fairly new, old and very ancient, which I suppose looking back did me more good than harm in my learning process, though at the time I did not think so.

Referring back to my school days our learning was so basic that no wonder it was called elementary. We were taught to read, write, measure and count money so that we could make sure our wages were correct, that was about it at one time. There was also a turnover of teachers going to or coming back from the war, which was very unsettling for all of us. One morning at assembly there stood out the front of the school a very tall, very smart, new, young, headmaster, who, we subsequently learned, was waiting to be called up into the Air Force. He turned out to be a very modern up to date teacher who had us enthralled with his stories, ranging from all about the universe to heroes and heroines of the war.

This first lesson at evening classes is, in some way for me, history repeating itself because about forty odd years ago my teacher then said, "Write me a story," just as the teacher has this evening.

I remember to this day what my story was because once I had started to write it seemed as though I could not stop. It took me every spare minute of three days to complete. I even gave up playtimes to continue writing. It was about an army sergeant gunner who became a hero by staying at his post and overcoming the enemy. It was so well thought of that I was advised to send it to an evening paper for publication. I never did myself but I often wondered if any other person took the trouble to.

That wonderful teacher who fired my imagination so much later became a pilot in the Royal Air Force and was shot down and killed earning a gallantry medal.

RMS

P.S. I am now old and retired with several grandchildren who I try to inspire to greater things than their Grandad ever achieved.

Life

Maybe!

I love to sit in my old armchair and leave my mind to wander

To let it roam to where it will, then just sit and ponder,

On things I have done and things I have seen and words I have said and shouldn't,

Of deeds and words that ought to have been said and now wonder why I couldn't,

I could have made speeches; held many meetings and pushed myself to the fore;

And just on a whim I could have sent for my plane and promptly flew on a world tour,

I could have been rich and owned lots of shares with people to do as I ask;

A very large house with walls all round and servants for the smallest task,

A leader of this; a captain of that and at least a knight of the realm,

A noble Lord a peer amongst men with a strong hand on the helm,

I could have rode horses; plotted many courses; been consulted by noble grandees

They would have been nice, taken my advice and paid me enormous fees,

If for a title I yearned, and could have probably earned by mixing with men in high places;

But to make quite sure of my station in life; I should have spent more days at the races,

Though it seems to me as I ponder away and dream in my old armchair;

That my life so far has been pretty good and on the whole quite fair,

I could have had glory and fame and wealth and positions of power in the land;

But good health I've had for all of my life; and that's something that cannot be planned.

My Old Home Town

I stood and wept an inward tear
And as I stood it became quite clear,
That my old home town had been passed by;
And then there escaped another sigh,
For my boyhood days not too long gone;
When doors and windows gleamed and shone,
When people came and spent and went
About their busy shopping bent,
The shelves were full of goods galore
With personal service and only one door,
With every hour there came a bus
Which stopped and turned at the terminus
When passengers alighted and smiled and talked
And around the town together walked,
The cars that came parked in the street
And stayed e're long no clock to beat,
So little time had gone it seemed
Since the shops were full and the pavements teemed,
And still I stood so full of sadness
At a different form of motorway madness;
The kind that takes the traffic by
To leave towns like mine to lay and die.

Up The Gills

This is the winter of our content
At last we have top management
The proof is there upon the field
The moves are bold the players skilled
For year after year we have waited the day
To stand in admiration as we watch the play
For this Gills side is tops for me
A better one I have yet to see
Surely this team deserves higher ranking
Up to the second div, we are all banking
So come on everyone, players, fans and all
United we stand, divided we fall
Let's make it the season we move on up
And perhaps next year we will win the cup
We thank you much for all the thrills
And we all say UP THE GILLS.

An Ode to Our Evening Class English Teacher

Our meeting tho' not clandestine,
Thursday sheer pleasure from seven till nine,
You have taught us much with kindness and care,
Your bubbly personality so very rare,
You have a lovely knack of getting through,
To a thicky like me and others too.
Our grammar you've corrected,
Our spelling you've connected,
The placing of commas especially inverted,
Of colons and full stops we are fully alerted.
'Tis with much regret I say goodbye,
I know now when to say lay or lie,
To write a great deal instead of a lot,
And much more than I learned when I was a tot.
Specially for myself as well as the rest,
I thank you much; you are one of the best.

All About My Nose

As you know my nose is now clear,
In a pub I can now smell the beer,
But I'm very afraid the surgeon has made;
A mistake, so it now sheds a tear.

You knows I knows lots about noses,
I hope I can now smell the roses,
But what if I can't and life takes a new slant,
And all I can smell are my toeses.

Fun

The Pigeon Who Could Not Find Home

The pigeon who could not find home
To find his way back was a pain,
On being released from the basket en route
He booked a return on the train.

As a racer he wasn't much good
He even got lost in a wood,
He preferred to fly not too far away
But stay in his own neighbourhood.

The pigeon who didn't fit the bill
To fly a long way made him ill,
He would much rather stay closer to home
And cuddle his girlfriend Lil'.

The pigeon who could not find home
Took his bearings from the local church dome,
When he last looked down to see where he was
He was over the Vatican, Rome.

The pigeon who could not steer right,
To help, had a couple in flight,
But it made matters worse, he drank far too much
And finished up high as a kite.

The pigeon who could not find home
Lost his way and started to roam
He dropped in to a garden to have a good rest
And was pointed the way by a gnome.

The pigeon who could not find home
Went for a flight all alone,
As a training run it wasn't much fun
So had a pint in the Dog and Bone.

In the end he found it a bore
Found his love on a far away shore,
He courted her day and well into the night
And never came home any more.

The moral of this story is
For birds who keep losing their way
Do your very best, keep persevering
It's much worse being a pigeon of clay.

The Hippo Who Doesn't Like Mud

I am the hippo who cannot wallow;
With thick black mud I can't cope,
I prefer to lie in a nice warm bath
Up to my eyeballs in soap.

I am the hippo who cannot wallow;
To be clean looms large in my life,
My family have warned me to mend my ways
Or I will never attract a nice wife.

I once courted a lovely lady;
A beauty I saw from first time,
But her idea of makeup
Was to wallow in thick black slime.

I am the hippo who cannot wallow;
Sorry! but I just don't like mud,
While my peers submerge in some nasty foul gunge
I like to swim in a pool in the nud'.

I am the hippo who doesn't like mud;
My daddy thinks I am rum,
His idea of luxury
Is wallowing in a lake of foul scum.

My friends all think I'm unusual;
Because to wallow to them is the ritz,
But to me all that filthy thick mud
Is the downright absolute pits.

I am the hippo who cannot wallow;
So my deodorant lasts all day long,
When they eventually climb out of that awful muck
My pals all tell me I pong.

To wallow is a family pleasure;
For a hippo an absolute must,
But to lay and play in that terrible filth
Fills me with utter disgust.

The Unhappy Mole

He was not happy about having to dig holes
The little mole who would rather climb poles,
It was not only the dark that he didn't like
But the dirt in his jam butty rolls,

He worked early shift in the morning
Clocking on when the day was dawning,
But long before the end of his spell
He was spending the whole time yawning.

Being a mole in the dark below ground
Digging a bit then throwing up a mound,
He didn't like the job at all
It nearly drove him up the wall.

He was always dirty, stank of mould
All the time feeling the cold,
Dirt in his fur, a broken nail
All sorts of muck in his beautiful tail.

Beautiful tail! bushy and brown!
The older moles noticed and started to frown
Different in colour, in a bad mood
He didn't look like one of their brood

When underground on hands and knees
How he longed for the chance to climb tall trees,
Or scramble easily up a pole
Where everyone could see he wasn't a mole.

He was no good at digging earth
Because he was a squirrel by birth
When now he looks down from high above ground
He smiles to himself when he sees those earth mounds.

The Elephant With a Memory Problem

I'm the elephant who cannot remember,
I'm the jumbo who's as thick as a plank;
When told to get other side of the pond,
I walked on the water and sank.

I'm the elephant who cannot remember,
Whatever I'm told doesn't stick;
I keep asking my Dad the time of day,
And he say's "Clear off, you get on my wick."

I'm the elephant who cannot remember,
With a brain of cotton wool in my head;
I wish, I wish I could remember my name,
That's why I'm called Jumbo and not Fred.

I'm the elephant who cannot remember,
I'm the jumbo who goes out in the rain;
I cannot remember to put a hat on my head,
So the water gets into my brain.

I’m the elephant who cannot remember,
I forget things as soon as they’re said;
I’m the jumbo who cannot remember the time,
To remember to get out of bed.

I’m the elephant who cannot remember,
My thinking is next door to none;
I cannot remember my birthday,
And that’s why I’m still only one.

I’m the elephant who cannot remember,
To smile at the folk in the zoo;
I need a constant reminder,
To lift up my trunk and blow thro’.

Family

A Proud Grandad

This is the story of a proud Grandad
Who even of an age thinks “I’m a lucky lad”
I have six grandchildren of whom I’m very proud
Of whom I can’t help but blow the trumpet loud

I love them dearly but the years are flying by
As I watch them grow, there escapes a sigh
Of satisfaction with their progress so far
You can be sure of this, it’s way above par

They are healthy and quick and very alert
Both boys and girls, so alive so pert
They are so full of life, full beyond measure
My heart is bursting with pride and with pleasure

I will tell you their names now one by one
These beautiful children of my daughter and son
And of course I must mention their spouse and mate
Without them of course there’d be nought to relate

First there is Layla so tall and so bright
A beautiful girl in everyones light
She’s twelve years old and growing up fast
No doubts about her, her future is cast

She is good at games and clever at school
I have no doubts about her future at all
She’s top in her class and draws with some skill
If her brains don’t get her there, her personality will

Next comes Nathan all of ten years old
Whose skill with a ball is there to behold
The loves of his life are football and art
But with all of his lessons he still plays his part

Good looking like Mum, athletic like Dad
He has every chance and they can’t be bad
Of being a star in more than one field
He has lots of talent on which to build

Lovely is Sally, the next in line
Growing up fast like an elegant vine
Tall and slim with dark glossy hair
Eight years old and beyond compare

So good at school with a very sharp brain
Like Mum and Dad so they can't complain
Good looking but with mind and will of her own
A future leader the seeds are sown

Damian is six with an innocent face
Don't be deceived he's quite a hard case
Angelic to look at but energetic and tough
Quite capable of taking the smooth and the rough

Content with himself doesn't mind being alone
Of nature he's interested, across fields likes to roam
When the time comes to make his way
He won't be found wanting at the end of the day

The next lad is Tim, alert and alive
Quite grown up and all of five
To him life is dramatic, black and white
No half measures but he'll be alright

He talks a lot and very fast
I'm sure his enthusiasm will last
He just can't wait to get to school
And when he does he will show them all

Last but not least by any means
Dear Katy of two who's full of beans
I read her a story as she sits on my knee
And I wonder what she will grow up to be

Somebody important you can be sure
She's as clever and sharp as a girl of four
I know she will make it to the very top
Her whole life before her noone can stop

That's the story so far, as I said "I'm very proud"
And as I sit and wonder aloud
I pray to God I will still have the spark
To take an interest as they make their mark

Six super children all of them grand
Who will make their living across the land
But wherever they go, to climb whatever hill
They will make old Grandad prouder still.

Mischief Is

Mischief is two sparkling eyes,
Two mobile legs and hands that rise
As high as they can surely reach;
To grab an apple or a peach,
Whatever takes his eye, the more
He feels has to climb up high for,
No danger, no fear are in those eyes
Just mischief and a love of life.

Mischief is a smile that says, you will
Love me though your thoughts could kill,
For all the mischief that he makes,
If he wasn't there our hearts would break;
He teases sister takes her toys,
He knows that we know how that annoys,
To him it's just a game to play,
To pass the time, the hour, the day.

Mischief is a tousled head
That looks up to you to give the lead;
The nod of approval, the shake of no,
Whatever it is you can bet he'll go
To do his own thing, he will be hell bent,
And for us to find which way he went;
Quick as a flash he's over the gate
And up the lane at a hell of a rate.

Mischief is a quickfire brain
That takes him out into the rain,
To walk all through the puddles 'til
His feet are soaked and he'll catch chill;
One little slip when Mum forgets,
The backdoor is open and out he steps,
Without a backward glance he's gone
Making for the nearest pond.

Mischief is a tot of two
With beguiling smile that says to you;
Hate me if you can or dare
But you know that I know
you have to share,
Your love with me and sister Sal;
You can look at me and say "That's him"
Because mischief is a boy named Tim.

Sweet Sally

Sweet Sally is our pride and joy;
She runs and shouts just like a boy,
In fact; at a glance; you just might think;
The colour for her is just not pink,
But big bold colours like green and black;
Cos life for her is there to attack,
But look more closely into her smile;
There you will see the feminine guile,
The screwed up nose, the crafty grin;
Just one brief smile, and you are in,
Her spiders web of female charm;
That in mens hearts will cause alarm,
Meanwhile as she grows apace;
Yorkshire will love her style and grace,
Nan and Grandad will glow with pride;
Until she is a bonny bride,
Cos she'll grow up a lovely gal;
Because she is our own sweet Sal.

A Rumm'un

He was four years old was our young Tim,
When we drove north to visit him,
"Come for my birthday," to his Nanny he cried,
With accent thick he couldn't hide,
As his Mum and Dad from south had flown,
No other accent had he known,
A Yorkshire lad, no accident of birth,
All life to him is joy and mirth,
He talks and talks and talks all day,
And to stop him in mid track I'd say,
"Ee by gum you're a rumm'un",

But on translation from North to South,
With accent thick from out of his mouth,
He would say to his Mum what Grandad said,
"Ee by gum your a woman".

Yorkshire

To walk the lengths and breadths of Yorkshire
That's what I would like to do
To climb the fells the dingley dells
And admire the lovely views
To stand on top of Pen-y-ghent
Look north, look west, look east
To gaze around for miles and miles
And give my eyes a feast
The beauty that surrounds you
Can take your breath away
I stood in awe on Pen-y-ghent
No words could I find to say
The words that came could not describe
The beauty that I scanned
Never in a million years
Could it be built by human hands.

A Hymn For My Gran

It seems only a few years span,
When I used to sing to my dear old gran,
She was wrinkled and grey and wise in her ways,
She used to prefer the old hymns of praise,
But her favourite of all was carols at Christmas,
Of 'Royal David' and King Wenceslas,
With my face washed and my pajamas on,
I would sit in her room all those years gone,
And sing my heart out in my boys treble voice,
She loved it when I sang the hymns of her choice,
'There is a green hill far away',
Or the well loved, 'At the end of the day',
At the end of my solos it was always my role,
To sing 'Jesu' lover of my soul',
This she loved dearly and never tired,
Of hearing me sing was her hearts desire,
Now, when in our local church we sing,
Those hymns of old with a bold ring,
I remember my Gran and those days long gone,
And the solos I sang to her alone.

Royal

Born to be King

The man who is to be our King
Has won himself a wife,
To him a wife though she may be
To us a Queen for life.

We have watched him grow from royal birth
Of royal blood may be,
But Charles to us is one of us
Despite his family tree.

He has chosen well and with great care
The lovely Lady Di'
And when he weds on the twenty-ninth
The whole country will be there.

Like him she has won the people's hearts
Like him she is well respected,
And when they are our King and Queen
We will all feel well connected.

As royals go he is the tops
There is no doubt at all,

That when the time that will has come
He will answer the country's call.

If ever a man was born to rule
In bearing, compassion and nature,
That man is Charles the Prince of Wales
Already a man of stature.

We have watched him grow from boy to man
As though one of our family,
And Lady Di' will be just the same
One of our family tree.

Our country needs a royal line
Our history proves it's worth,
And with the bond it ties for us
We'll resist any power on earth.

Whether from within or from without
To undermine this nation,
That power will have to break this bond
Of us and our royal relation.

Our reigning Queen who is loved by all
Must be very proud of her son,
The man who was born to be our king
Who lady Di' has won.

I Wonder

It's very early on the Wedding Day
As I sit in my old armchair
I sit and ponder on the big day
Of her Majesty's son and heir

She's carried the worries and cares of state
For a very very long time
I wonder how her son will rate
When they log the Royal line

He's very popular with everyone
And has a very outgoing nature
But when the big time really comes
Will he have the guts and stature

From what we have seen as we've watched him grow
From babe to boy to manhood
As I sit and ponder in my old armchair
I think he'll be very good

From now on in it will begin to show
If he's as good as his Royal Ma
For up until now he's had lots of luck
For he's leaned on Mountbatten and Pa

Now he has Di to look after as well
As well as his Royal duty
I can't help wondering as I sit in my chair
Can he tear himself away from her beauty

He could be tempted to say to himself
After today's big thrash
Is it all worthwhile for Di and I
Or shall I do an Edward and dash

I don't think he will, between you and me
For he knows he's loved and respected
He'll stay the course like his well revered Mum
His duty will not be neglected

When they do come to write the history books
Of Prince Charles and his lovely Bride
They'll recall that this was the era when
Great Britain regained all its pride.

Twelve Years Later

Twelve long years have gone by
Since the magnificent wedding of Charles and Di'
Eventful years have come and gone
Now Charles and Di' are on their own.

I'm still sitting here all alone
Wondering where it all went wrong,
Handsome Prince, beautiful Princess,
Why oh why! wasn't it a success.

My television did not lie to me
I saw them take vows and agree
To be married for life, for evermore
And each other forever adore.

People came from afar to witness and see
Some were born high, and some lowly like me,
But one thing in common we all had
We were happy for them and very glad.

We prayed for them as they knelt at the altar
To be brave and strong and never falter,
We wanted so much for them to succeed
To be King and Queen in our time of need.

Queen Elizabeth, bless her, will not always be here
How the royal line will follow is not very clear,
We needed them to wear the crown
We cannot help feeling we have been let down.

It seemed so positive when we saw them married
Who amongst us would have carried
The slightest doubt that they would stay
To reign over us till their dying day.

As I sit and ponder in my old armchair
I cannot help wondering if they really care,
They have really hurt us their loyal subjects
Or are we all just royal rejects.

A Sad Sunday Morning

I am still sitting here in my old armchair
My dream long gone of yesteryear,
Of Charles and Diana our King and Queen
The most loved royals the world has ever seen,
My dream shattered by their divorce
Their marriage not meant to stay the course,
And now this morning, something far worse
Could there be a royal curse,
For Diana is dead, killed in a crash
Was this meant to be a backlash,
A punishment for our great sin
Of not protecting her as she should have been,
Her Royal Highness, her title by right
She would then still have been our one bright light,
Our royal family having gone adrift
She alone gave us all a lift,
Now she is gone, so young yet so strong
Leaving a weeping, mourning throng,
In life more loyal with loving care
In death more royal than others dare,

A short span of time, a world bereft
Where is our icon, we who are left,
We weep for her sons, one our future King
We pray that some solace our weeping will bring,
For we all now claim that Diana belonged to us
But whilst alive did we make that much fuss,
Did we truly deserve such a lady for our Queen
Should we dare think of what might have been.

Tim's Visit

It was not the fact that he actually came
But the distance he travelled put others to shame,
Two hundred miles on his own he braved
Paying his fare on pocket money saved,
It's not often the young have time for the old
The lad is worth his weight in gold,
A long weekend of not doing much
Because Grandad had to rely on a crutch,
Uncanny for a lad of his age, he knew
What a visit to us from him would do,
With my leg in plaster, not getting around
For several weeks I have been housebound
Although it was a bad time of the week
The mourning for Diana was at its peak,
Nevertheless for us sheer pleasure
When we look back, a time we will treasure,
For a young man with so little time to be had
He found a whole weekend for his Nan and Grandad.

Love

Everlasting Love

It was up and it was running
For our love was overflowing,
We were wild and indiscreet
But no matter, we would meet.
Nothing kept us, nothing stopped us
Our love was extra, over, plus,
We were young, she very tender
I was on a mad mad bender,
She gave me all, she felt she must
Mine was a hard ferocious lust.
It must end, we must stop
But it went on and on, over the top,
I wanted her, she gave way
We needed each other night and day,
I took her used her, made her pay
Mad for her in every way,
Hers was a love of give and trust
Mine was a selfish animal lust.
Teenagers then, now we are old
Love and lust has turned to gold,

We have been married now for fifty years
Years of happiness and many tears,
I have tried and tried to be kind and nice
I must have succeeded more than once or twice,
I love her still tenderly so
She still fulfills me, makes me glow.
My thoughts plague me now of being alone
May God call me first so that I may atone.

Men Like You

May I say to you my dearest Ju' how much I really care;
I look at you from head to toe; you've got a lovely pair,
Of eyes my dear, what did you think that I was going to say;
You have a lovely pair of legs of course,
I always think that way,
I would like to mention your eyes again;
For they are green and grey,
And when I look into them;
They look back at me and say;
You can look at me and you may touch,
But what I feel, depends how much,
You may kiss my cheek and hold my arm,
But you get to me with your old world charm;
I'm all yours as you well know,
Because I really love you so,
But do you love and really care, for me so much
And not my lovely pair,
Although you look into them deep,
Are you going to keep, your promises to me,
And when I've given myself to you,
Will you disappear into the blue;
My mum has warned me of men like you.

Miss.Capon Regrets

I do regret Miss.Capon;
I like to bet Miss.Capon,
I am in debt Miss.Capon;
I cannot marry you.

It is with sorrow Miss.Capon;
I have to borrow Miss.Capon,
I'm going to jail Miss.Capon;
I cannot marry you.

I cannot pay Miss.Capon;
They'll take me away Miss.Capon
For a long stay Miss.Capon
I cannot marry you.

Please may I say Miss.Capon;
Don't run away Miss.Capon;
On another day Miss.Capon,
I will marry you.

You are my pal Miss.Capon;
A lovely gal Miss.Capon;
Waiting is hell Miss.Capon;
So will you marry me.

I am now free Miss.Capon;
Do you love me Miss.Capon;
Can I borrow the fee Miss.Capon,
So I can marry you.

I am the said, Miss.Capon;
The very rich Miss.Capon,
And I'm going to stay Miss.Capon,
So I will marry you.

Heavenly Choice

Darling, if I am ever asked how our marriage endured for so long when many many others have fallen apart, I shall reply;

"I married an angel."

If any of our grandsons ever ask me how they can make sure their marriages work,

I shall tell them;

"Make sure you marry an angel."

Our Golden wedding anniversary is getting quite close and people will most surely be asking,

"How is it you have never been apart?"

My answer will always be,

"I married an angel."

It has been said that whilst other couples, old as well as the young, have loud rows and long arguments ours sails serenely on with hardly a ripple, my response to that is,

"I married an angel."

When the children were young and money was short you went out to work at all types of menial jobs like domestic cleaning and working in the fields to be able to buy those little extras. By then of course I already knew I had,

“married an angel”.

There were times when my work kept me away from home many many hours sometimes days. But no matter how long or short I had been away you were always, and still are, there to greet me on my return smiling, neat and tidy and nicely groomed, because of course,

“I married an angel.”

After a night out with the lads and arriving home in the early hours a bit the worse for wear. No recriminations, no sour expressions, just a coffee and a serene you;

“The angel I am married to.”

In the past when life has disheartened me and I have been very down; it was you who I turned to, so calm and understanding, the

“Angel I am married to.”

After my recent operation, with my leg in plaster and unable to get about much, there you were administering to my every need, cooking the meals, waiting on me hand and foot, literally no fuss no bother because you are the

“Angel I am married to.”

When shortly we celebrate our Golden wedding anniversary, inevitably the same old question will be asked, how? and of course there is only one answer,

“I married an Angel.”

But I know that you were once asked, in this day and age of divorces and separations and taking partners instead of spouses, how do you stay so close? And without hesitation you replied,

“I married a saint.”

Rate For The Job

This is the story of my dear spouse,
Who cleans and dusts around the house,
All day she washes, cleans and sews,
How much she is worth nobody knows,
Because I never pay her,

She scrambles eggs and bakes a cake,
Then up the stairs the beds to make,
The washing is needed day by day,
I've no idea how much to pay,
Cos I really can't afford her.

Out to the garden the cats to shoo,
Into the bathroom to clean the loo,
Down on her knees to clean the grate,
I'm glad she's not aware of the going rate,
Cos I really can't afford her.

Out comes the needle to mend a skirt,
Then the iron to press my shirt,
The housework, humdrum day by day,
I hope I'm never asked to pay,
Cos I really can't afford her.

The hoovering's done, the house is clean,
Just as it has always been,
On goes the oven; out comes the flour,
I'm pleased she isn't paid by the hour,
Cos I really couldn't afford her.

Out to the market to shop for food,
Never ever in a bad mood,
Back home in kitchen kettle on,
To make some tea for her dear Ron,
All I can do for all her endeavour,
Is promise to love her for ever and ever.

www.ingramcontent.com/pod-product-compliance
Ingram Content Group UK Ltd.
Pitfield, Milton Keynes, MK11 3LW, UK
UKHW041925190726
13854UKWH00003B/1449

9 781847 992574